BareBackPress

This is a work of fiction. The characters, incidents, and dialogue are the products of the author's imagination and are not to be construed as real. Any resemblance to actual events or person, living or dead, is entirely coincidental.

BareBackPress
Hamilton, Ontario, Canada
For enquiries visit www.barebackpress.com
Cover art by Anton Berkasov
Cover design by Karina Bush

ISBN-13: 978-1926449234
ISBN-10: 1926449231

CONTENTS

Plugged-In ~ 1
Temple ~ 2
Cloud I ~ 3
Unspoken Words ~ 4
Cloud II ~ 5
Claws ~ 6
Cloud III ~ 7
Maybe ~ 8
Cloud IV ~ 9
RIP ~ 10
The Order ~ 11
Sutra Of The Computer Body ~ 12
Cloud V ~ 20
Disease ~ 21
Nature Rolls ~ 22
Pith ~ 23
Mine ~ 24
Ashes ~ 25
Secrets ~ 26
Cloud VI ~ 27
The Tint ~ 28
Taste It ~ 29
Repeated ~ 30
Cloud VII ~ 31
His Furs ~ 32
Act I ~ 33
Four Faces ~ 35
Familiar ~ 36
Cloud VIII ~ 37

Lifeform ~ 39
Easy ~ 40
Apex ~ 41
Human ~ 42
Cloud IX ~ 43
Karma Man ~ 44
Cloud X ~ 45
Exit ~ 46

To my mentors

"If a man could pass through Paradise in a dream, and have a flower presented to him as a pledge that his soul had really been there, and if he found that flower in his hand when he awoke ~ Aye! and what then?"

Samuel Taylor Coleridge

B R A I N   L A C E
//

PLUGGED-IN

The machine stirs
The camera is on

Yes

His male brooding
One of those dark
Plugged-in souls

At each end – wasteland
This discontent
Our breeding ground

I'm pouring wine over the laptop keys
Down the wires
To intoxicate you
To fuck with you
Dressed up for you
I'm infiltrating
Your stress is visible

TEMPLE

Bleach my cunt
The spinning vortex
Of slut crystals
That started all this

You are a little brain slut
And your cunt is in your brain
Where your conscience should be

Slut crystals spinning
Edges shredding
Unnecessary head cells

I often wake up choking
Need no blockage
Inject bleach into my brain
Wipe the disc

CLOUD

Why do I dream of it?
Always before
A big dream with
A Beast versus a Horse
Dragged by the neck
Off its seat
It waits
Ready to run
Nothing it can do
It waits

Why do I dream of it?
Always before
The Horse barely contained
Cracking the walls of its enclosure
The Tragic Horse of Romance
Why do I lie down?
On the road
Waiting for hooves

UNSPOKEN WORDS

My throat burns
With unspoken words
Pushed back into my tissue
They don’t belong there
They didn’t belong in the world either

So they gather

CLOUD

Seed to flower to seed
To flower to seed to flower

The great lotus
Feeding chain

Navel to brain to navel
To brain to navel to brain

He bares a man inanimate
Needing fed

A promise of ecstasy
Is made

Probing his dissonance
It pollinates

Back
Seed to brain to seed

CLAWS

He swears
He didn't think it

Claws

Were already growing
Out of my ribs
No going back
Can't take back a thought
Hyperpink bitch extensions
Spraying out of my gut
Clawing for the thoughtform
I think I'm stronger
Than my self-control

CLOUD

I should be at work
Window open
This hot satin afternoon
Room evaporates into

Milk on the breeze

The tree trunk
Expands and contracts

My ribcage
Expands and contracts

Paradise
Where the trees give milk
In return for nothing

Milk the tree
Milk the tree
Milking the tree
Milking it
Up and down
In my best earnest
Milk on satin
Is the exquisite dress
To sleep in
Afternoon

MAYBE

A bed so fertile
We can drink from it
Eat from it
Live off of it

Fuck and talk
The essential into creation
Thrive in lover's health

Maybe
The Gods underneath
Will reward us
With self-sufficiency
The ones who dripfeed
Off of base
We have plenty of it

IV
CLOUD

I had a dream
You were bleeding from the gut
She was nursing you
I was driving the bus

You are trying to make it stop
Fighting
Tight
Twisting
Tight
In your torso
Down to your cock
It's all in your head
In a crevice
At the source of it
Light

RIP

Little girls
If you played with Barbie
Listen to this
You'll want it
You'll beg a higher power
You've been
Biologically programmed
To be driven over
By a truck-man
It's so fucking romantic
You'll rip your fucking hair out
You'll stand outside yourself
Some long bastard night
The ejaculating painball
On that bed
Is you

THE ORDER

With these fingers
I could change everything
Write a few words to
Begin the order required to
Reset the universe

Close our eyes tight
The order enters
The cogs of the machine
Promises to process our promises
Yes I take your promises
Nobody gets hurt
In this version

SUTRA OF THE COMPUTER BODY

Talk to me
In night talk

We have different feelers
In the dark

An open
Space to detach

Sending them out
Through my forehead

My millipedes
On your electrical cords

Licking the drive
Saliva on their bellies

One by one
Find yours

Your black zero
Black zeroes

Say something

Both hands
There

X: awake?
K: Yes.

A spray
Of nerve endings

X: why aren't you sleeping?

The darkness is full of language

K: I can't. The usual. Restless.

Speaking lace
Words wrap abstracted

X: me too. and tense.

Read the lace
Not the words

K: My chest pains are back.

Words delay
Their form

X: you are too delicate

Tendrils of lace
First we mesh

K: I'm fine.

Two
Multiplying hungry thoughts

X: tell me more. you're being vanilla.

Seeking out
The innermost privacies

K: I'm boiling with something unknown. I could smash up my apartment tonight.

We develop seamlessly
Keep us like this

X: tell me.

I want hours
So I can dissect it

K: No.
X: brat

Breathing hot LCD

K: Did you read that email?
X: yes it is solicitous. are you going to reply? flirt with him?

Child of love
Glued
To the confusing
Sensation of you

K: I have no urge to flirt with anyone.
X: you should.

ASMR escalating

K: I'm not like you, I'm not whoring myself around. I don't need the attention.
X: i like it when you take out your claws

An abyss
Sex mess

K: Dick.

Drunk cortex
Sutra of the Computer Body

K: I had a snake dream.
X: tell me about it

Holding all our love inside
In code
In fragments
In memory

K: The second snake dream in a week where I beat it to death. This time it couldn't be killed. A cobra. I don't understand it and it pisses me off.

The sewers of our minds
Sutra of the Computer Body

X: who or what is the snake, do you think?

Who addicted who?
Sutra of the Computer Body

K: Could be someone impure.
X: could be.

Two-headed one
Sutra of the Computer Body

X: go to somewhere we can IM

Sleeping lotus
Shakes herself awake

K: OK.

Jets of lace
Meat in lace

Entering the deep mind state

Skin as the endless patterns
Of the sun
On a body of water
Helix of light

His kind words
Male sweetness

My brain fizz
Feeling it thousand-fold

K: Something wrong with my connection. Fucking internet.

And silence doing this to me

X: this is exhausting. you are exhausting.
K: Brat if I do. Brat if I don't.

Imagination blows
A hole

X: i'm aggravated
K: You deserve it.

Petal in rapture

X: it's a terrible waste. like tossing a flower away into a trash bin.
K: You're not making sense.

In the aftermoment
I almost admitted it

X: It's all so much.
https://www.youtube.com/watch?v=vMTEtDBHGY4

We must back off

K: So beautiful.

Don’t want this to sleep

X: no flesh, just words.

There are eggs
Thousands of eggs
Under us
You are a fertile man

K: Who is being dramatic now?

Bury in the parasites now

X: no more. talk soon.

Prisoner of erasure
Sutra of the Computer Body

K: OK goodnight.

Our tendrils retract
Into our bodies static

Will he come back to me
The same version?

I hear only the old
Dead echo of lace

I fuck his echo

CLOUD

We met again last night
Outside the doctor's office
I'm trying to tell myself
We need to see a doctor about this
It's a sickness
It was nice to see you
We smiled at each other
Nothing more
Didn't feel toxic
But by fuck it is

DISEASE

Sitting there
Cock hard
For whore
Not me
This is
Whore disease
Rising – flying
My tongue is hot
About to say something it shouldn't
Instead I get on my knees
Adapt my behavior
Clean up the cum
Generated by another

/

Nature rolls in ecstasy
Abandoned - pure
This is the strongest desire

PITH

A hundred men in one of his hairs
He doesn't know

There's barely one man
In most men

He is a city
Built on rivers

Bites his lip
Brain calculating
Like a fiend

Can't predict
His move

His men penetrate
Down to my pith
Make me want to grow younger
So I can regrow
Become new to him
Never bore them
So I can grow
A hundred women in me

MINE

I could take you in flight
Snatch you off her
Her grip is thin

Stand you stripped
In my forest
Pinned in by my wings
My land is an expanse

See all of you finally
Your beautiful dick
Mine to be sublimated
You wouldn't run

It is ours

Integrity won't
Help you forget

Few men
Touch an angel
They created

ASHES

A grey wall
Between us
Frames of decay

Sinking into a thought
I don't want to accept

While my body is young
Ripe in the midday sun
An urge to burn
Unbearable suchness

In the ashes
In the quantum
When our bodies
Finally break down

The matter between us
Will not exist

The oceans
The wrong turns
The deeds

Meanwhile

We miss all the love
Its impermanence

/

When I was a girl
I observed
The secrets adults keep
I could see life
More vivid in the hush
Life is

VI
CLOUD

I tried to speak
My mouth filled with love

I spoke flowers
Pouring out of my mouth

He kissed me
I filled him up with them

They will each fruit over time
He will know my love

When the final flower fruits
I will flower him again

For eternity I will perpetuate us
And we will perpetuate eternity

THE TINT

Months of
Fuck blur

When this flush leaves us
When the tint lifts
When we can feel again
Something outside of this

We'll walk through the remains
Look what it took
To immortalise urgency

We turned to stone
At him and her
As stone you crush

And their hearts were mortal
Mashable flesh

TASTE IT

You slither around your life
With her

Picture perfect

Fracture - surprise

Inside your head
You're up to your neck
Gonna taste it soon

Bad
Old
Man

The tits in your mouth tonight
Aren't mine
Aren't pouring
A tempest
Into you

You
Poor
Little
Bastard

Being fed from the wrong species

REPEATED

In my head
Fuck You
Too much
Three days ago

I visualised cutting
The cord that attaches us
With big garden shears
Hacked at it
After I cut it off me
Hacked at thin air
Too much
Three days ago

Tonight
You are softly floating
On the outside of my brain

You're pining too

I can't rewind you
Back into the ether
The cord re-formed taut
You haven't exhausted

VII
CLOUD

The water under me
Fills with spiders
Adult black females
They've been sleeping
In the nothing
They are impatient
They will mate

Giant pornographic beauties
In the bath
Widespread legs
Watching you on a screen
The colour runs
It's mating season
I'm going under
Steep with them
Float in the din

HIS FURS

Head on my wall
He is the other
He climbed the golden mountain

I am the archer
And the arrow

His furs
Draped on my furniture

Blonde on his furs
Stroke his furs
Blondes evolved for this
To stun his eyes
To inspire
To catch
The alpha male
For the best share

ACT I

In my bardo
I watched the sex act
At the membrane

Everyone who came before
Came by the act
In the act

I watched
A young man
A young woman
Tilted
In love

Made in love
Of love and of milk

Organs made of
A pump of milk

Hidden tubes
Carriers of love

From the father
To the mother
From the mother
To the infant
Mine to him

You must
Beat his balls
with sharp objects
Until he cries and cries
your name
Cries trying to clutch at you
for comfort
Someone stays adrift
in their bardo
His sperm drips out
of the slice
and

He is calm
He is on my breast now

FOUR FACES

In our domesticity

1. Bastard you
2. Ugly me

Our darkest positioning

I wanted to stay beautiful forever
You are malforming me

3. Nice you
4. Nice me

Drunken slaves
Our boat sails
In mirrored rivers
We throb perverse
The four of us

FAMILIAR

Muted by your lonely grasping
I could fall too
Melting into sadness
Is a familiar bliss

Is he
In flux or a mess
A lover or catalyst

Go back in time
Back through the fibres of being
You know the whole
How it holds us

Torment flows
Is not concrete

Sort it

This is an expectation
I will not cling
I've spilled my disgrace plenty

VIII

CLOUD

In a car park
I'm in the back
Behind you
Put my hand
Around your seat to you

Your fingers are cold
Cold interplay

No eye contact
Locked in strange permissions

I know your fingers
Imprints of your voice

Holding
Holding
The slowest coldest fuck

Birds growing in the car body
I hear them in the cavities
In the engine
In distress
Trying to compel

Birds growing in the body
Because we are holding hands

Wings beating off the metal
Prints like our hands trapped

Prints like my mouth
In my fingerprints

LIFEFORM

Our love is our baby
The baby we'll never have
A hundred years ago
We'd have fourteen kids
You'd come home
Hands and feet black
To a room full of love

Our love was a foetus
Pink glowing angel mix of us
You put it inside me
To incubate
A digital lifeform
I could see through my skin

The birth was hard
It's in our hands
Sometimes mine
Sometimes yours
Sometimes both
We have dreams for it
Perfections
But
It cries

EASY

His kisses taste like sex
Still

When I get ready
My every choice

Of beauty
or words

Still now

His kisses taste like sex
Still now

Every move I make
Dictated by it

APEX

We're in
Arms and eyes and mouths
And Lawyer talk
Cyst in the pit of my liver
With teeth
And little cunt ducts flexing
Acid projectile
Come down
You're bankrupt
Give me the peak

Man saying sad words
Trying to keep me

I know how God feels
In receipt of
All those
Private prayers
At night

HUMAN

I know I've made you
So angry
You hate me
I'm aroused
First time
I've done this
To someone
I've had it done to me
Taken years off my life
Unrecognisable state
I want you
To answer my question

Can you bring the human
Out of another person
Beyond capacities
The inner deformity
The freak you keep
In your attic
And ever look at them
The same again?

CLOUD IX

You look so peaceful
Supine weak in my dream
I put my mouth on yours
You think I'm going to kiss you
I can’t do that
In the warm space
I spoke into your mouth
From the outside it looked like a kiss
Spoke every vile hate thought
You've brought up in me
Every one
A whisper from an abusive mother
To a child she wishes she never had
Isn't she so loving to him
Kissing him slow so deliberate
Telling the child he is worthless
And he ruined my life

KARMA MAN

Living my karma
Via you

I asked to be degenerate
And life brought
Your constant dissolution

I chose my
Innate ability to harm myself
Can learn every lesson but this selfish
Drive to have the spectrum
Of intense

Like karma
My punishment memory
Is long
When your time comes
Don't cry for sympathy
You picked first
You were fully grown
You entered our vow to
Execute sufficient misery

CLOUD X

You
Hungry you
Stalking me
Pulling me from my body
Into the great void
Where the creature of us
Spins our love

For what?

And you
Gentle you
Making contact
Quiet and guardian-like
Inducing the half-state
Of hope

For what?

Analyse the signs
The old teachers say

Maybe dreams lie
As much as you

EXIT

You are this distant spark
Darkling fountain
Spitting blues
From the exposed end
Of a broken cord
Untamed from the hotel wall
Too dangerous to touch your source

I'm starting to see
The other side from here

Truth more vital
than any passion
evades me

Exit this space

There is nothing
Left to grow

Seeds spread rot

Let me sleep
In my flower cup

Acknowledgements

The author would like to thank the following publications where some of these poems originally appeared: 48th Street Press, Bold Monkey, Horror Sleaze Trash and Squawk Back.

About the Author

Karina is an Irish writer, born in Belfast and now living in Rome. She is the author of three books, 'BRAIN LACE' (BareBackPress, 2018), '50 EURO' (BareBackPress, 2017), and 'MAIDEN' (48th Street Press, 2016). She is currently finishing up a collection of short stories set in Belfast and writing her first play. For more visit her website karinabush.com.

Also by the Author

Maiden
50 EURO

BareBackPress

www.barebackpress.com

Hamilton, Canada

12974779R00038

Printed in Great Britain
by Amazon